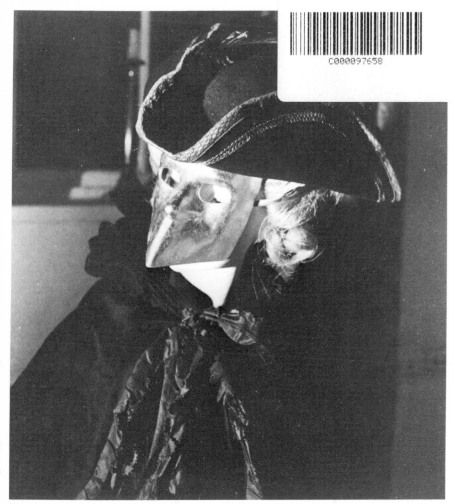

Venetian carnival mask and nineteenth-century domino. This mask is of recent date, but whether gilded as in this instance, or black or white, the designs have changed very little since the eighteenth century. They were based on those used by the characters in the Commedia dell'Arte and can be seen in the many paintings of Pietro Longhi (1702-85) of the Venetian Carnival.

FANCY DRESS

Anthea Jarvis and Patricia Raine

Shire Publications Ltd

CONTENTS

Set in 9 on 9 point Times roman and printed in Great Britain by C. I. Thomas & Sons (Haverfordwest) Ltd, Press Buildings, Merlins Bridge, Haverfordwest.

COVER: *Arc-en-Ciel (The Rainbow), a hand-coloured engraving from 'Travestissements', P. Robin, c 1868. This charming design for fancy dress entitled 'The Rainbow' has used the wide crinoline of the mid 1860s to clever effect. The overskirt of ruched grey fabric, cloud-like in appearance, is splattered with darker spots of grey to represent the raindrops. Drawn back, it reveals the freshness of the flowers after rain with a rainbow arching over them. The rainbow colours are repeated around the tops of the boots and the rainbow tiara has an aigrette sprinkled with pearls.*

British Library Cataloguing in Publication Data
Jarvis, Anthea
    Fancy dress.—(Shire albums; 127)
    1. Costume—History
    I. Title II. Raine, Patricia
    391'.8 GT1750

ISBN 0-85263-698-9

ACKNOWLEDGEMENTS
    The authors gratefully acknowledge all the help and encouragement they have received from private owners, libraries and the many museums visited, which directly or indirectly have assisted the writing of this book. In particular they wish to thank Mr Richard Robson, Curator, Costume Galleries, Castle Howard; Mrs Pat Clegg, Director of Harrogate Museums Service, formerly Keeper of Costume, The Castle Museum, York; Mr Charles Stewart; the staff of the Royal Archives and the Royal Library, Windsor Castle; Mrs Anthea Bickley, Keeper of History, Bradford Art Galleries and Museums; Mr Robin Harcourt Williams, Librarian and Archivist to the Marquess of Salisbury; Mrs Joan Kendall, Head of Textile Conservation, Hatfield House; Mr John Brandler, Mrs Brenda Falconer and Mrs Sheila Garnett. They would also like to thank the staff of Bermans and Nathans; of the Art and Design Library, Liverpool Polytechnic; of the Reference and Local Studies Libraries, Central Library, Hull; and of the Photographic Department, Merseyside County Museums. Acknowledgements to reproduce illustrations is made as follows: by gracious permission of Her Majesty the Queen, pages 7 (top), 11 (left and right), 12 (top); by kind permission of the Marquess of Salisbury, 27 (bottom), 28 (top left); Bermans and Nathans, 30; Bradford Art Galleries and Museums, 20; Castle Howard Costume Galleries, 1, 16 (left and right), 18 (right); Mrs Sheila Garnett, 24 (left); Hull Central Library, 27 (top), 28 (bottom); *Hull Daily Mail,* 31 (bottom); Liverpool Polytechnic Library, Liddell Hart Collection, 4 (left and right); Merseyside County Museums, 28 (top right); National Portrait Gallery, 10 (bottom); Mr Charles Stewart, 7 (bottom right), 13 (left and right); Victoria and Albert Museum, 6, 10 (top), 15 (left and right), 17; The Castle Museum, York, 7 (left).

LEFT: *Henry VIII, not dated. This person has chosen a character for which his figure is eminently suited. It is a very elaborate fancy dress and in all probability would have been hired.*
RIGHT: *Father Time, 1909 — on roller skates! This illustrates that novelty is certainly not a prerogative of our own time. Much earlier — in 1877 — a masquerade ball on wheels was held in Nottingham, and the commentary in 'The Graphic' said it was 'as far as we are aware, a novel idea'. In contrast to wheels, blades were frequently donned to propel masqueraders round ice rinks. The earliest such occasion reported in the 'Illustrated London News' was in 1870 when Prince Arthur visited Canada.*

INTRODUCTION

What is the age-old appeal of fancy dress? For some, it has granted a wish, like a fairy godmother's wand, enabling a suburban housewife to be Cleopatra, a bank clerk Henry VIII or an eighteenth-century duchess to be a milkmaid. For others it has offered, by the casting off of the clothes and conventions of the work-day world, the opportunity to be truly themselves. For those in search of romance, comedy and drama, fancy dress offers great potential, as writers and dramatists have always found. For everyone, it is a harmless, legal, and quite delightful way of being 'different' for a night.

3

LEFT: *Habit of a Nobleman of England in 1640: from 'A Collection of the Dresses of Different Nations, both Antient and Modern' Volume 2, by Thomas Jefferys, published in 1757 as a pattern book to provide masqueraders with ideas for costumes. 'Vandyke' costumes were very popular with masqueraders as a result of the romantic interest taken in the age of Charles I, and the picturesque splendour of the fashions as portrayed by the court painter Anthony Van Dyck.*
RIGHT: *Habit of the Grand Seignior or Emperor of the Turks, in 1700: from Volume 1 of Thomas Jefferys's 'A Collection of the Dresses of Different Nations'. Turkish costume, introduced to England in the early eighteenth century by English visitors to Constantinople, was extremely popular as masquerade dress for both men and women. Some masqueraders wore genuine Turkish robes, others hired Turkish outfits from a masquerade warehouse, and yet others might contrive their own 'Turkish robes' by embellishing their own fashionable clothes.*

CARNIVALS AND MASQUERADES

Dressing up and the wearing of masks and fancy disguises has been associated with the celebration of festivals in Europe over many centuries, but modern fancy dress in Britain owes its origin principally to the seventeenth-century Italian carnival. In Venice and the other major Italian cities, in the weeks preceding Lent, masked revelry took place nightly in the streets. The participants, of all classes, wore masks and either fanciful decorative costumes or voluminous dark cloaks called dominoes. Troupes of musicians and street actors performed before the revellers, and there could be decorated floats, dancing and fireworks.

In the eighteenth century, 'masking' or masquerading was introduced as a public entertainment in England, the first masquerades being organised by a Swiss, Count Heidegger, at the King's Theatre, Haymarket, around 1710. Londoners eagerly took to these colourful entertainments, where they promenaded in masks and costumes, danced, listened to music and partook of supper. Because of the anonymity the masks gave, manners could be informal, behaviour free, and flirtations and assignations not only possible but probable.

English masquerades became more like their Italian parent when, from the 1730s onwards, they were held outdoors in the summer at the public pleasure gardens around London, especially at Ranelagh in Chelsea, and Vauxhall Gardens in Lambeth. In 1772 the building of the Pantheon in Oxford Street provided an indoor winter venue where subscription masquerades were held. These were supposedly more select and therefore more desirable than their predecessors, and this initiated a decade when the masquerade was at the peak of its popularity. Nevertheless, the impossibility of keeping the masquerade exclusive, and the licentiousness and intrigue that inevitably accompanied it, led to its rapid decline at the close of the eighteenth century. By then it was out of tune with the new mood of a society preoccupied with wars abroad and the industrial revolution at home.

Looking at prints of the eighteenth-century masquerade, it is apparent that though many chose to wear the Italian domino or cloak over fashionable evening dress, many others chose outfits of great diversity and originality. Among the most popular costumes were those particularly associated with the Italian Carnival, the Commedia dell' Arte characters Harlequin, Columbine, Pulcinella and Pantaloon. Their highly stylised costumes are still with us today, as the ever popular Harlequin, Pierrot and Clown. Other patterns for costumes were the fashions of the past — those of the Charles I period, as seen in Van Dyck's portraits, had a particular fascination. Also used were the exotic and romantic fashions of the Orient, Africa and North America, all places only just becoming available to the British traveller and therefore subjects of much wonder and curiosity. Many chose 'low life' or character costumes, such as comic countrymen (especially Scots), savages, madmen, chimney sweeps, sailors, and old women (men in 'drag'). Others chose costumes satirising the latest fashions, or current political events, or which poked fun at establishment figures such as politicians, clergymen and lawyers.

Very few masquerade costumes have survived; those that were elaborately made and decorated and covered with jewels would have been taken to pieces and recycled after the event, and others would have been clever improvisations for the one occasion only. The spirit of masquerade costume survives best in the letters, diaries and novels of the period, and in portraits of the nobility and gentry, who sometimes chose to be recorded for posterity in their costumes — attesting to the high degree of elegance, fashion and popularity attained by the masquerade in its heyday.

FANCY DRESS IN THE ROMANTIC AGE

Although the masquerade had fallen from favour in the early years of the nineteenth century, the love of fancy dress had by no means diminished. Private masquerades, or as they came to be increasingly called, fancy balls, were given by leading society families, and by London clubs for their members and guests, especially at times of national celebration such as the victory of Waterloo. Unlike the masquerade, where the participants were masked and incognito, at a fancy ball masks were not usually worn and the emphasis was on the attractiveness and inventiveness of the costume chosen. This made the latter much more acceptable to the higher moral tone and greater restraint that society was beginning to adopt.

For the fancy ball goer of the 1820s and 1830s the choice of character and costume was much influenced by the romantic preoccupations of the age. One of these was an intense interest in Britain's past; the obsession with the pageantry and chivalry of the middle ages, and the 'Merrie England' of the Tudors, was partly a reaction against the growing

A hand-coloured engraving from a set of eight plates illustrating 'contres danses' from 'Étrennes à Terpsichore', Paris, 1815. In this set of dancers can be recognised the early nineteenth-century concept of Scottish Highland dress, both male and female; two peasant costumes, one perhaps Greek as the Greek key pattern decorates the apron, the other with the large hat possibly Swiss; a Commedia dell'Arte Pierrot and a medieval lady.

industrialisation and attendant squalor of the time. The novelist Sir Walter Scott appealed to and fostered this mood with his immensely popular novels, set mainly in Tudor Britain and in eighteenth-century Scotland at the time of the Jacobite uprisings. As a result, Scott's heroes and heroines, both historical and fictitious, were among the most popular of those chosen for fancy dress. Mary, Queen of Scots, from *The Abbot,* Rebecca and Rowena from *Ivanhoe*, Rob Roy and Di Vernon from *Rob Roy*, Amy Robsart and the Earl of Leicester from *Kenilworth*, and Lucy Ashton from *The Bride of Lammermoor* appeared again and again, often with several impersonations at the same ball. Fancy balls were even given devoted entirely to the theme of Scott's novels, such as the Ivanhoe Ball given in Brussels in 1823 by the Prince and Princess of Orange. As an alternative to Scott, another source of heroes and villains that appealed to the Romantic Age was the plays of Shakespeare, the characters of Romeo and Juliet, Hamlet, Shylock and Richard III finding many

willing impersonators.

There were also contemporary romantic heroes with whom people eagerly identified themselves. The ideals of liberty, nationalism and personal freedom, new in the 1770s, had now spread throughout Europe. The new hero of the early nineteenth century was the peasant leader or the native chief, who inspired his people to defend their land and liberty against foreign oppressors. The ideal embodiment of this heroic role was Tecumseh, a Shawnee chief. An ally of the British in the American War of 1812, he was later seen in popular British imagination as the impossibly brave, noble but doomed hero, fighting to the death for the rights and freedom of his tribe. At the Liverpool Fancy Ball held in 1830 in the Town Hall, at least fifteen men chose to wear Red Indian costume, two impersonating Tecumseh.

The popularity of European travel with the British aristocracy in the late eighteenth century led to an increased interest in the scenery, architecture and the native costumes of such countries as Spain,

6

TOP RIGHT: *Alexandra, Princess of Wales, as Mary, Queen of Scots, dressed for the Waverley Ball, held at Willis's Rooms, July 1871. More appropriately to represent a costume of the mid sixteenth century, the dress incorporates the outline of the mid 1860s rather than the fashionable bustle of the early 1870s. A costume in the Museum of London could be this dress remodelled in the Venetian style and worn at the Marlborough House Ball three years later.*

BOTTOM RIGHT: *Mrs Edmund Davenport as Mary, Queen of Scots, late 1870s. The exact date of the event for which this dress was worn is not known, but the pose, which shows a bustle being worn, and the hairstyle are evidence for the suggested date. This costume and that worn by the Princess of Wales have many points of similarity, such as types and use of fabric, the form of decoration and style of sleeves, head-dress, yoke and ruffs.*

LEFT: *Di Vernon, about the 1880s. Of all Sir Walter Scott's heroines probably the most popular throughout the nineteenth century was Di Vernon — 'the heath-bell of Cheviot and the blossom of the Border' — in the novel 'Rob Roy'. She seemed to embody all the attributes which the young Victorian woman would have most liked to emulate, but which the dictates of society made her unlikely to achieve. This costume is made from dark green velvet, with waistcoat and facings of red facecloth, and trimmed with silver braid and buttons.*

Costume for DI VERNON, heroine of ROB ROY, by SIR WALTER SCOTT
Based on the riding costume of the period   of Louis XIV
CASTLE MUSEUM, YORK

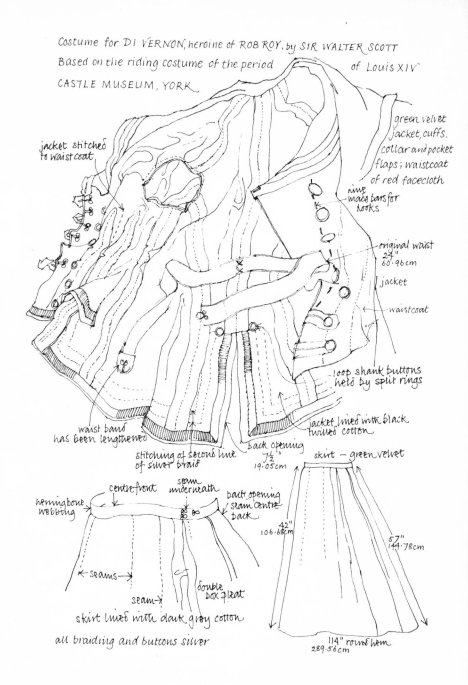

jacket stitched to waistcoat

green velvet jacket, cuffs, collar and pocket flaps; waistcoat of red facecloth

rings made bars for hooks

original waist 24" 60·96cm

jacket

waistcoat

loop shank buttons held by split rings

jacket lined with black twilled cotton

waist band has been lengthened

stitching of second line of silver braid

back opening 7½" 19·05cm

skirt — green velvet

centre front

seam underneath

back opening seam centre back

herringbone webbing

42" 106·68cm

57" 144·78cm

seams

seam

double box pleat

skirt lined with dark grey cotton

all braiding and buttons silver

114" round hem 289·56cm

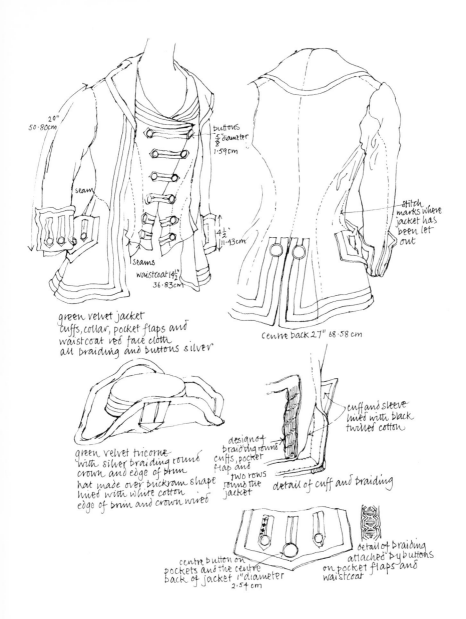

20"
50·80cm

seam

buttons
$\frac{5}{8}$" diameter
1·59cm

seams
waistcoat 14½"
36·83cm

4½"
11·43cm

stitch marks where jacket has been let out

Centre back 27" 68·58 cm

green velvet jacket
cuffs, collar, pocket flaps and
waistcoat red face cloth
all braiding and buttons silver

green velvet tricorne
with silver braiding round
crown and edge of brim
hat made over buckram shape
lined with white cotton
edge of brim and crown wired

cuff and sleeve lined with black twilled cotton

design of braiding round cuffs, pocket flap and two rows round the jacket

detail of cuff and braiding

centre button on pockets and the centre back of jacket 1" diameter 2·54 cm

detail of braiding attached by buttons on pocket flaps and waistcoat

ABOVE AND OPPOSITE: *These details of cut and construction of the Di Vernon costume, illustrated on page 7, enable it to be dated to about the 1880s and show it is not a riding costume of a much earlier date as had previously been thought.*

9

ABOVE: *Two guests at a fancy dress ball giving alms to a poor woman — hand-coloured lithograph, French, about 1840. It is difficult to decide what the costume of the young lady actually represents; maybe an abstract concept such as 'Summer' or 'Queen of Flowers'. The young man is a débardeur and, to the left of the picture, framed in the doorway, is a débardeuse. A débardeur is a stevedore or docker and a débardeuse is 'a woman's fancy dress in imitation of a longshore-man's costume, popular in the nineteenth century', the style of which at that period must have been considered quite daring.*

RIGHT: *George Gordon, sixth Lord Byron, by Thomas Phillips, after 1835. This portrait of Lord Byron in Albanian costume is a smaller version of the upper part of one painted by the same artist in 1813, omitting the white kilt worn with the richly embroidered jacket. That Byron considered it useful as fancy dress is shown by the fact that he would have lent it to John Murray as such, but 'his wardrobe was out of town', and in a letter to Margaret Mercer Elphinstone accompanying the costume he describes how to wear and adapt it, and suggests 'it will do for a masquerade'.*

Italy and Switzerland. Books illustrated with engravings of such costumes were eagerly seized on as sources of fancy dress. To dress as an Italian peasant gave the upper class English girl the opportunity of wearing a charming picturesque costume, and of displaying fashionable democratic tendencies (albeit vague ones) as well. The European country that held by far the greatest attraction for the Romantic Age was Greece. It combined the glamour and cruelty of the Orient with the idealism of a small country fighting for its freedom from the corrupt Ottoman Empire.

The enormous success of Lord Byron's poetry was the result of his adoption of the same potent ingredients; Oriental exoticism, violent death, tragic love, and above all, the proud, moody and cynical hero. On his first visit to Greece in 1809, Byron bought himself several Albanian costumes. Although he never wore them in England, except to sit for his portrait, his reputation, the portrait, and his poems combined to make Greek dress enormously popular as a fancy dress costume. Many hundreds of men and women in the 1820s and 1830s went to fancy balls dressed as Circassians, Albanians, Greek pirates, Turkish Pashas, Corsairs, Greek slave girls and Brides of Abydos.

Sketches, drawn by Queen Victoria in her Journal, of Prince Albert as Edward III and herself as Queen Philippa, dressed for their first Bal Costumé, 12th May 1842. As part of the nineteenth-century revival of 'medievalism', no happier choice could have been made by Queen Victoria and Prince Albert than to represent 'the noble-hearted and tender' Philippa of Hainault and her husband Edward III, the founder of England's oldest order of chivalry. Nor could a more suitable costume adviser have been found than James Robinson Planché, dramatist, costume historian, antiquarian and heraldic expert. The Queen expressed her desire that the costumes should be historical and strictly accurate. Planché based them on those of the effigies of Edward III and Queen Philippa in Westminster Abbey.

ABOVE: *A sketch taken from Queen Victoria's Journal of Prince Albert, Queen Victoria and Charles, Prince of Leiningen, dressed for the Bal Costumé, 13th June 1851. The Queen and the Prince Consort did not impersonate any particular historical characters at this their third and last costume ball, the theme of which was the Restoration. Their costumes, again devised by Planché, were based on the fashionable dress introduced by Charles II from the French court of Louis XIV. Queen Victoria's costume, which is the only one of hers to survive from any of the costume balls, is now in the Museum of London. It is of rich grey watered silk trimmed with gold and silver lace and ornamented with rosettes and loops of pink ribbon, originally fastened by bouquets of diamonds.*

LEFT: *Engraved fashion plate from 'Journal des Demoiselles', January 1861. Here three children are shown in fancy dress; the eldest wearing a costume based on the Russian sarafan, the young girl as Harlequinette and the boy in a costume most probably Bulgarian, but, if not, one with definite eastern influence. The girls' dresses were both fashionable in shape, being worn over crinolines.*

LEFT: *Major Charles Talbot Davenport dressed in Chinese robes for a fancy dress ball, 1879. With the rapid development of Far Eastern trade in the nineteenth century, it was inevitable that many original costumes would be brought back to Britain by both businessmen and visitors. Many men who disliked the idea of fancy costume nevertheless would consider wearing genuine exotic dress such as the superbly embroidered and colourful silk garments of Mandarin China.*
RIGHT: *Mrs C. T. Davenport as 'The White Cat', 1879. Fancy dress based on characters in fairy stories became very popular in the later nineteenth century, particularly with children, probably because of the great success of the spectacular pantomimes produced in London at this period. 'The White Cat', a fairy story from the collection of Madame d'Aulnoy, is not familiar to children today, though the character still appears as the partner of Puss-in-Boots at the wedding of Princess Aurora in the ballet 'The Sleeping Beauty'.*

QUEEN VICTORIA DRESSES UP

As a proof of how much the moral climate surrounding the fancy dress ball had been elevated and improved since the eighteenth-century masquerade, in the early 1840s Queen Victoria and Prince Albert were enthusiastic promoters of fancy dress balls at Buckingham Palace. Popular taste had by now largely abandoned exotic foreign costume, and to dress up as a Circassian slave or a Red Indian was thought by the early Victorians to be rather immodest and unrefined. The vogue was all for historical subjects and characters. Victoria and Albert gave a 'Plantagenet Ball' in 1842, set in the court of Edward III, but with a small sprinkling of other historical periods allowed; a *Bal Poudré* set in the mid eighteenth century in 1845, and a 'Restoration Ball' in 1851. The Queen and Prince took a very serious interest in the costumes and accessories, which they wanted as authentic as possible, and commissioned the costume historian, J. R. Planché to design them; the whole exercise being seen as a serious exercise in historical research as well as a pleasurable occasion. The royal couple's costumes were extremely sumptuous, being embellished with jewels and antique lace, and were recorded for posterity in portraits by the Queen's favourite artists Sir Edwin Landseer and F. X. Winterhalter.

Encouraged by the Queen's enthusiasm, fancy dress balls achieved a new popularity in the mid nineteenth century, held by clubs and societies in public halls, as civic celebrations by mayors in town halls, and as part of the Christmas festivities by families at home. The emphasis continued to be on historical characters and costumes, which were considered to be in better taste than exotic or humorous ones. In 1863 the Mayor of Liverpool gave a 'Fancy Ball' in the Town Hall to celebrate the visit of the Channel Fleet to the Mersey. In the *Commemorative Record* of the ball the writer adopts an earnest, slightly pompous tone, 'The scene . . . was more than gay, it was splendid. No fancy dress ball was ever more so; and in none were violations of taste so few . . . or objectionably peculiar characters so entirely absent'.

The vast majority of these tasteful costumes were based on historical styles, and the period now most favoured was the eighteenth century. From literature, various suitable characters could be found. Shakespeare provided Romeo and Juliet, Beatrice, Portia and Shylock; Scott's heroes and heroines were still in favour and characters from Longfellow's and Tennyson's poems and Dickens's novels made their appearance. Many young ladies chose to go dressed as peasant girls 'from countries where the poor dress picturesquely', as such costumes could be colourful and piquant, and offered excellent opportunities for displaying their charms.

Another popular choice for ladies at this ball, and a type that had appeared only rarely hitherto, was the emblematic or allegorical costume. No less than twenty-two ladies chose to go dressed as Night, and in addition, 'Summer, Autumn, Winter, Spring, Snow, The Last Rose of Summer, Morning, Harvest, Undine, Midnight, Ceres, Fleurette and many other characters spread an atmosphere of poetic fancy over the scene.' Ladies were probably encouraged to choose costumes like these by their dressmakers, as they could be based on the most fashionable evening dress, embellished with every sort of trimming, artistic, fanciful and sumptuous, and the resulting creation served as an excellent advertisement for the dressmaker's skill and taste.

Ideas for costumes for the fancy balls of the 1860s seem to have been gleaned from a wide variety of sources, and any book or collection of prints that offered suggestions was eagerly utilised. Women's magazines such as *The Englishwoman's Domestic Magazine* and the *Journal des Demoiselles* regularly published coloured illustrations of fancy dress costumes, with descriptions of materials and accessories. Prints of actors and actresses in 'period' or peasant costumes from popular plays or ballets were another source of inspiration, as were books on travel and exploration, with illustrations of native costumes. The epithet 'very correct' was used as a term of high praise in descriptions of fancy dress of this period, and complete authenticity was aimed at by people wearing various types of native dress, which returned to fashion in the 1870s. The opening up of trade with Japan made Japanese robes popular, and in 1883 Red Indian costume reappeared spectacularly at the Savage Club Ball in the Albert Hall. The central feature was a band of Redskin warriors, who performed a Buffalo Dance, and whose costumes were the result of meticulous research. Descriptions of individual costumes in the press even quoted the particular engraving in Catlin's *North American Indians* from which they were copied. The result was both spectacular and strictly authentic, and thus a complete success in mid-Victorian eyes.

LEFT: *Mrs Arthur Paget as Cleopatra at the Devonshire House Ball, July 1897. Mrs. Paget's costume, made by Worth, was described in 'The Queen' as having 'a train of black crêpe de chine, embroidered with gold scarabaeus and lined with cloth of gold; the skirt of black gauze, worked with lotus flowers in gold; the bodice, glittering with gold and diamonds, was held up on the shoulders with straps of large emeralds and diamonds; the square head-dress was of Egyptian cloth of gold, the sphinx-like side pieces being striped with black and gold and encrusted with diamonds'.*

RIGHT: *The Duchess of Devonshire as Zenobia, Queen of Palmyra, July 1897. The Duchess took part in a 'Procession of the Orientals', composed of some of the fabled queens and kings of the ancient world, and her dress was said to be 'a marvel of soft tissues and exquisite ornament'. The skirt was of gold tissue, embroidered in emeralds, sapphires and diamonds, which opened to show an underdress of cream crêpe de chine, embroidered in silver, gold and pearls and sprinkled with diamonds. The bodice was of gold tissue, with a stomacher of diamonds, rubies and emeralds. A gold crown, encrusted with the same jewels, had a diamond drop at each curved end and, in the middle, two white ostrich feathers.*

EDWARDIAN EXTRAVAGANZA

In the last quarter of the nineteenth century, the fancy dress ball came to be regarded as quite the most appropriate way to celebrate special events, both public and family ones, and the ideal way for ambitious hostesses to make their mark in Society. Really big fancy dress balls were always widely reported in the press, and the expense and lavishness of some of them, especially in America, made headline news. Alva Vanderbilt, wife of the American millionaire William Vanderbilt, gave a fancy dress ball as a housewarming at her new home, the Marble House, in 1883. Costing a quarter of a million dollars, it was probably the most lavish party given up to that time in America.

In England too, the fashion was growing for grand fancy dress balls to be held during the London Season. Queen Victoria herself never took part in fancy dress events after the death of Albert in 1861, but her son and daughter-in-law,

15

LEFT: *Roman matron, early twentieth century. This costume consists of a tunica and pella (cloak) in a loose-weave fabric of silk and cotton mix, trimmed with gold braid, and decorated with the Greek anthemion or honeysuckle design, machine embroidered. A gold laurel wreath and gold kid sandals complete the fancy dress. Little Greek or Roman costume features in illustrations of the nineteenth-century fancy dress balls, probably because classical dress bore very little or no relationship to fashionable female dress and was therefore difficult to adapt.*

RIGHT: *Polish court costume, 1913. This costume by Paquin, made for Lady Borthwick, later the eighth Duchess of Grafton, is a splendid example of couture fancy dress. It is of turquoise satin, woven with a velvet floral pattern outlined with cord. The style is of an open trained surcoat with hanging sleeves, trimmed with ermine down the centre front, round the hem and round the opening of the sleeves. The centre front of the bodice and silk underskirt are covered with silk gauze, both embroidered with silver and lavishly beaded. A wired halo-shaped head-dress of cloth of silver, overlaid with silver lace and encrusted with pearls and turquoise coloured stones, completes the costume.*

the Prince and Princess of Wales, carried on the royal tradition by holding a fancy dress ball at Marlborough House in 1874. They were also the guests of honour at the famous Devonshire House Ball, given by the Duke and Duchess of Devonshire to celebrate the Diamond Jubilee of 1897. The seven hundred guests were asked to come dressed as a famous person from history. Souvenir books were published illustrated with photographs of all the better-known guests in costume, so it has become one of the best recorded fancy dress events ever. Some of the 'famous people from history' were characters more from fable and legend than from true history, but that gave more scope for gorgeous and exotic costumes. Most of these were made by the leading London and Paris couturiers

Sir Harry Stonor as Lohengrin, July 1897. As a member of one of the foremost English recusant families, which could be traced back to the twelfth century, his ancestry contained medieval chivalry and religious fervour, making the legendary character of Lohengrin a particularly suitable one for him. Here in chain-mail armour, tabard and winged helmet, and with sword, shield and hunting horn, he is dressed for his part in the quadrille of chivalry at the Devonshire House Ball.

LEFT: *Hand-coloured engraving from 'La Mode Illustrée', 1880. The characters portrayed here are Folly, Incroyable and a young bride or bridesmaid. The dress for Folly, like many others, traces its ancestry back to the costumes worn by the characters in the Commedia dell'Arte. The differences between Folly and Harlequin are found in the styles of head-dress, Folly wearing a pointed cap and Harlequin wearing a bicorne, while the points of the skirt and cap are belled for Folly and not for Harlequin. Incroyable was the name given to men who wore the exaggerated fashions of the Directoire period in France, and the name was later given to an adaptation of their costume worn by women as fancy dress.*

RIGHT: *Folly costume, 1913. This beautiful French Folly costume is made from white ribbed and blue silk, edged with silver braid and trimmed with bells. It consists of a separate skirt and bodice, cap, and a folly doll made to match the outfit, unusual in that it has survived with the costume. The skirt is made up from ten rows of overlapping triangles, getting progressively larger towards the hem, and in each row the triangles are of blue and white silk alternately and all are attached to an underskirt, this arrangement giving the traditional diamond pattern. The maker's name and address — Mme Didier, 32 Rue de Laborde, Paris — is printed on the waistband of the bodice.*

Castle Howard Costume Galleries

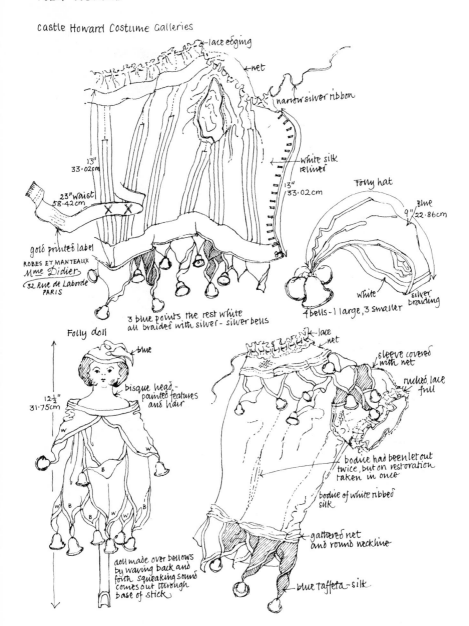

lace edging

net

narrow silver ribbon

white silk reliner

13"
33·02cm

23" waist
58·42cm

13"
33·02cm

gold printed label

ROBES ET MANTEAUX
Mme Didier
32 Rue de Laborde
PARIS

3 blue points, the rest white
all braided with silver - silver bells

Folly hat

Blue
9"/22·86cm

white

silver braiding

4 bells - 1 large, 3 smaller

Folly doll

blue

bisque head -
painted features
and hair

12½"
31·75cm

w

B

w   B

B   w   w   B

doll made over bellows
by waving back and
forth squeaking sound
comes out through
base of stick

lace

net

sleeve covered
with net

ruched lace
frill

bodice had been let out
twice, but on restoration
taken in once

bodice of white ribbed
silk

gathered net
and round neckline

blue taffeta - silk

Drawings showing the construction of the bodice of the Folly costume and hat shown on page 18 (right), and explaining one of the methods of making a Folly doll.

and dressmakers. The famous Jean Philippe Worth created a Louis XV court costume for the Duke of Marlborough at fabulous expense, and a Cleopatra costume for Mrs Arthur Paget. The Princess of Wales went as Marguerite of Valois, the Duchess of Connaught as Anne of Austria, and the host and hostess were the Emperor Charles V and Zenobia, Queen of Palmyra. Among the more dubiously historical characters were Lady Holford as Titania, Sir Harry Stonor as Lohengrin and Mrs Leonie Leslie as Brunhilde.

The great success of the Devonshire House Ball led to a series of similarly spectacular events organised by society ladies in the theatres and public halls of London in order to raise money for charities. Usually a particular theme or period was chosen. For example, a 'Shakespearean Ball' was held at the Albert Hall in 1911 in aid of a Shakespeare Memorial Theatre, and a 'Fête at Versailles' was held there in 1913 in aid of the Incorporated Soldiers and Sailors Help Society. All over the country fancy dress balls were held in assembly rooms and drill halls in aid of hospitals and orphanages, and numerous private balls and dances took place celebrating birthdays, engagements, and comings-of-age.

With so many fancy dress events in the social calendar, Edwardian ladies must frequently have had to grapple with the question of what they should wear. Fortunately, plenty of help and advice was available. The many women's papers, such as *The Queen*, *The Ladies Realm*, and *The Woman At Home* ran articles in nearly every issue over the winter season offering practical help and suggestions. Ardern Holt, in *The Queen*, found her readers anxious for original costumes and suggested, in the issue of 14th January 1893, 'A Piece of Artillery', 'An Easy Chair' (for a man of rather large proportions), 'The Front Hall' and 'Oysters and Champagne'. She could fairly claim to be an authority on fancy dress, being the author of the bestseller *Fancy Dresses Described, or What to Wear at Fancy Balls* which ran to six editions between 1879 and 1896.

This book was commissioned and pub-

The costume of Mrs Titus Salt as Mary, Queen of Scots, worn at the coming-out ball for her only daughter, October 1895. The dress was made by Simmons's, the well known court, fancy ball and theatrical costumier.

20

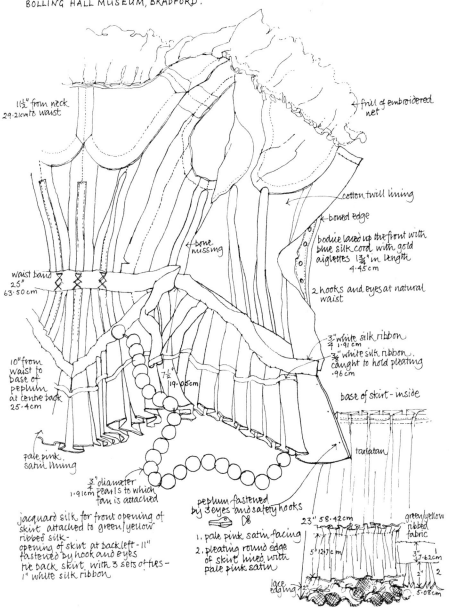

FANCY DRESS — MARY QUEEN OF SCOTS
Worn by Mrs. Titus Salt - widow of Titus Salt, 5th. son of Sir Titus Salt,
at the coming-out ball of her only daughter, Mary Isobel, age 19, in October, 1895.
BOLLING HALL MUSEUM, BRADFORD.

11½" from neck
29.21cmto waist

←frill of embroidered net

cotton twill lining

←boned edge

bodice laced up the front with blue silk cord with gold aiglettes 1¾" in length 4.45cm

2 hooks and eyes at natural waist

waist band 25" 63.50cm

10"from waist to base of peplum at centre back 25.4cm

←bone missing

¾" white silk ribbon 1.91cm
⅜" white silk ribbon caught to hold pleating .96cm

7½" 19.05cm

base of skirt - inside

tarlatan

pale pink satin lining

¾"diameter 1.91cm pearls to which fan is attached

peplum fastened by 3 eyes and safety hooks

1. pale pink satin facing
2. pleating round edge of skirt lined with pale pink satin

23" 58.42cm

green/yellow ribbed fabric

5" 12.7cm

3" 7.62cm

2" 2

lace edging 2"

5.08cm

jacquard silk for front opening of skirt attached to green/yellow ribbed silk-
opening of skirt at back left - 11" fastened by hook and eyes
the back skirt, with 3 sets of ties -
1" white silk ribbon

Drawings showing the elaborate cutting and intricate sewing which went into the making of Mrs Titus Salt's costume (page 20).

21

lished by Debenham and Freebody, who advertised that they would make to order any of the costumes described. Department stores and fashionable dressmakers alike competed for the fancy dress trade, as did the theatrical costumiers, who made costumes to order and kept large stocks for hire (especially of men's costumes) which offered an easy option for the unresourceful. The West End firm of L. and H. Nathan enjoyed royal patronage, and supplied the Prince of Wales with his outfit as the Grand Prior of the Order of St John of Jerusalem for the Devonshire House Ball. Their main rivals were the firm of Simmons's of Covent Garden, who had refined to an art the supply of costumes for fancy dress functions in the provinces. For Mrs Titus Salt's ball at Saltaire, Bradford, in 1895, they not only made Mrs Salt's own dress, but sent their catalogue to all her guests, and arranged a special showing of some of their choicest stock at one of Bradford's leading hotels, for their convenience. There was certainly much money spent and much to be made in the Edwardian fancy dress world.

'Joy of Life', an original design from the fashion house of W. W. Reville-Terry, about 1927. The costume, without the torch, wings and head-dress, is now in the collection of the Museum of Costume, Bath. It belonged to the Countess Brecknock, and until the original drawing came to light was thought to represent 'Flame'.

Participants in a fancy dress ball, about 1920. In addition to the usual complement of clowns, pierrots and the ever popular gypsy and Folly costumes, two costumes are of particular interest. The one on the extreme right represents the topical 'Kodak Girl' taken from the life-size cardboard cut-out figures seen for many years in camera shops. The figure on the far left is wearing a dress designed to represent Night and Day or Dawn. It is an adaptation of the fashionable barrel-skirted dress, its dark skirt suggesting the night sky, while the top of the bodice in contrasting fabric and the head-dress of splayed ostrich feathers together suggest dawn light and the rays of the rising sun.

FANCY DRESS IN THE JAZZ AGE

In the years immediately preceding the First World War the wearing of fancy dress reached near epidemic proportions. The anxieties and economies of wartime soon put a halt to its more frivolous aspects, though throughout the war pageants and *tableaux vivants* played an important part in raising funds for war charities. After the Armistice the prevailing mood of relief and euphoria demanded parties and yet more parties to try and forget the war's tragedies and horrors. Fancy dress was enthusiastically adopted by the 'bright young things' who were turning the social world topsy turvy by introducing all-night parties, jazz, cocktails, and all kinds of exhibitionist behaviour.

In the many memoirs and autobiographies written by socialites, statesmen, writers and artists who were young in the 1920s, fancy dress parties appear again and again. It was considered most important that the person's identity should be completely disguised, and his or her friends kept guessing as long as possible, and to this end people often changed into completely different outfits during the party or ball. Masks came back into favour and good taste, introduced by the Victorians, was thrown out of the window. Costumes had to be amusing, bizarre, or shocking to be a success. Elaborate team efforts were a new element; parties of friends dressed as cocks and hens, or as a pack of cards, and at one ball eight society ladies went dressed as the Eton College rowing eight, complete with boat. Theme parties were also very popular, such as the notorious 'Baby Party': 'anything from birth to school age' the invitations read. The guests, dressed

LEFT: *Black and White scotch whisky, mid 1930s. During the 1930s, the wearer of this costume, Laura Mitchell, regularly cruised to warmer climates for her health during the English winter and had this costume specially made for a shipboard fancy dress ball, which always was and still frequently is a highlight of a long distance sea voyage.*

RIGHT: *Yardley lavender girl, about 1919. As illustrated advertisements became more widespread early in the twentieth century, trade-mark figures became a frequent source of inspiration for fancy dress. In 1913, Yardley's adapted 'The Primrose Seller' from Francis Wheatley's 'Cries of London', changing the primroses into lavender to become the standard trade-mark for their lavender water. Advertising in 'Weldon's Fancy Dress for Ladies and Gentlemen' about 1936, Yardley's said they would make the beautiful frock of the lavender girl 'specially to fit you...at a nominal cost, made to measure from British made Art Silk, complete with Hat, Fichu, Apron, etc, a bouquet of artificial Lavender, and Basket if required'.*

as babies or children, arrived in perambulators, ran races on donkeys or scooters, and drank cocktails from nursery mugs. There were also 'Wild West Parties', 'Russian Parties' and 'Circus Parties', among others, most of which succeeded in attracting shocked criticism from the older generation and gleeful publicity from the newspapers.

There appeared to be no escape from fancy dress, for apart from private parties, which were given by all classes,

fancy dress dances took place in public halls, restaurants and clubs, and were considered an indispensable part of the holiday at any really smart hotel. They were also a popular feature of holiday cruises, which enjoyed a boom in the 1920s, and a suitable costume, or the basis of one, had to be planned with the rest of one's cruise outfit. Dressing up was also a very popular type of entertainment within the family, on Christmas Night or New Year's Eve, or to celebrate

24

birthdays or anniversaries. It was usually an impromptu affair, with costumes improvised from the family dressing up chest, its miscellaneous contents perhaps including some items originally made for amateur theatricals, some pieces of genuine native or foreign costume, and other remnants of a previous generation's finery. From these materials relations of all ages would disguise themselves as pirates, gypsies, Victorian ladies and other time-honoured characters, the very familiarity of the garments becoming part of the fun.

With so many occasions for fancy dress, it was natural that the commercial world would not be slow to profit from an obvious need. Many catalogues survive, issued by theatrical costumiers and department stores listing and illustrating, with prices, every type of costume which could be made to order or hired. A particularly enterprising firm was Weldon's, the paper pattern manufacturers, who issued catalogues of many hundreds of fancy dress patterns in the 1920s and 1930s, which were used extensively by the theatrical costumiers and professional firms as well as home dressmakers. Weldon's also showed considerable enterprise in foreseeing the potential of advertisements as fancy dress, especially those which featured a costumed figure as a trademark, such as the Ovaltine Lady,

Records, about 1936. On the right is a detail of a photograph taken at Blackpool, most probably of entrants for a fancy dress competition, and maybe not instantly recognisable as 'Records'. But their costumes follow, to the last detail, that of an illustration (left) with this title for a paper pattern in a Weldon's fancy dress catalogue, about 1936. In addition to the dresses with appliquéd designs of black discs, and conical hats with three rings of records, they each have a quaver on the shoulders, a choker with a quaver hanging from it, and ribbons round the upper arm, with notes attached.

851003
Records

Patterns
price 1s.
each.

the Quaker from Quaker Oats, and the Golly from Robertson's Marmalade, and arranging with such firms to retail patterns of the costumes. In addition, some firms offered to supply by post complete, made-to-measure outfits.

A look through Weldon's catalogues reveals that though many of the designs were based on old favourites like pierrots and clowns, national costumes, ladies and gentlemen of the olden time and the occasional well known historical character, many more reflected contemporary life, fashions and light entertainment. Apart from advertising, sources were popular song titles, characters from comics and cartoons, and, increasingly, the cinema. For the first time, the choice of costumes for fancy dress was based on a popular and classless culture, not an aristocratic or intellectual one.

CHILDREN'S FANCY DRESS

Although the children of eighteenth-century aristocratic families were occasionally dressed in 'fancy' costumes for a portrait — Gainsborough's *The Blue Boy* being the best known example — fancy dress parties were rare occurrences in the nursery world until the mid nineteenth century. Again, it was Queen Victoria who helped to make the idea more popular. She encouraged her own children to dress up and delighted in making watercolour sketches of them in their costumes.

The Queen and Prince Albert gave a 'Fancy Dress Children's Ball' at Buckingham Palace in 1859, and from the 1860s onwards many such functions were held, especially at Christmas, and often, like the adults' balls, with the purpose of raising money for charities. An important event in the world of juvenile fancy dress was the 'Fancy Dress Ball' at the Mansion House given by the Lady Mayoress of London in 1876. Although not immediately repeated, from 1883 onwards it became an annual event, and is still held today. Many of the mayors and civic leaders of other cities followed suit, and fancy dress balls were the obvious way to celebrate big national events. Queen Victoria's two jubilees were celebrated in this way, as was the Silver Wedding of the Prince and Princess of Wales in 1888, for which the Mayor and Mayoress of Leicester gave a children's fancy dress ball, commemorated in a presentation album containing 269 photographs of the children who were present.

Though much of the children's fancy dress was, like that for adults, purely frivolous and an excuse for a conspicuous display of wealth and social prestige, for some there could be an underlying educational purpose to it. The wearing of native dress of children from other countries helped foster the British child's interest in geography, and history could likewise be illustrated by dressing up as famous persons from the past. The Marchioness of Salisbury gave a 'Juvenile Fancy Dress Ball' at Hatfield House on New Year's Eve 1874, at which nearly all the child guests were dressed in Elizabethan costume. The magnificent setting of Hatfield's late sixteenth-century architecture and furnishings must have made it an unforgettable experience for the children, as if their ancestors had come to life again for the evening.

From illustrated newspaper reports of the juvenile fancy dress society events in the Edwardian period, it is evident that most of the children's costumes were elaborate, miniature versions of what was popular for adults. As such they were probably chosen with more regard to what the mother thought pretty and picturesque than to the child's comfort and convenience. Eighteenth-century court costume, complete with powdered wig and sword, was considered especially attractive for boys but not, one suspects, by the boys themselves, while for girls 'Dresden China Shepherdess' and 'Good Queen Bess', complete with ruff and farthingale, were two most uncomfortable but popular choices. Writing in the 1920s, more than one of these child guests recalled bitter memories of parties blighted by unmanageable finery which in their own eyes made them look ridiculous.

ABOVE: *Detail from the engraving in the Illustrated London News, January 1875, of the Marchioness of Salisbury's Juvenile Fancy Dress Ball at Hatfield House. Lewis Carroll was a house guest at Hatfield and wrote in a letter, 'I came yesterday, to be present at a children's fancy ball, which was a very pretty sight. The house is Elizabethan, so most of the dresses were of that period, the eldest girl, Maud, being dressed as Queen Elizabeth, and the ball began with a grand royal procession, which was very well done.'*

BELOW: *Costume originally worn by Lord Robert Cecil as the Spanish Ambassador to the court of Queen Elizabeth I, at the New Year's Eve children's fancy ball, 31st December 1874. The complete costume consisted of doublet, trunk hose, cape, hat, ruffs, sword, dagger, hose, garter and shoes; all have survived except the last three items.*

Perhaps as a result of this, most parents of the 1920s and 1930s were determined that their children should have costumes they enjoyed. Writers in women's magazines begged that the children should choose for themselves, and suggested nursery rhyme and fairytale characters, simple animal costumes, or characters from classics such as *Alice in Wonderland*, *Peter Pan*, or *Little Women*. For boys cowboy and Red Indian costumes established themselves as firm favourites, made even more popular by the 'Westerns' seen at children's Saturday matinée film shows. Weldon's fancy dress patterns especially catered for the mother dressmaker, who was more likely to want to make a cheap, colourful, robust costume than to strive after elaborate or artistic effects. Mothers were also urged to let the children help make their costumes, perhaps by cutting fringes or painting decorations. Cheapness became a posi-

27

ABOVE LEFT: *The fourth Marchioness of Salisbury with two of her grandchildren at the Tudor Revels, Hatfield, 1927. The costumes made for the children's New Year's Eve fancy ball were used on subsequent occasions. The Spanish Ambassador's costume can be seen here being worn by one of the pages. It was probably worn at the Hatfield Elizabethan Fête in May 1924; and there is a photograph of the Hon. Robert Palmer, nephew of Lord Robert Cecil, wearing the outfit in 1896.*

ABOVE RIGHT: *A bat: fancy dress outfit worn to the Lord Mayor's Children's Ball, Liverpool, January 1912. Like many small boys, the eight-year-old subject of this photograph hated having to wear uncomfortable, restrictive or 'sissy' clothes. His mother, therefore, very sensibly based his costume on the garments he liked wearing most, his school jersey, shorts, stockings and shoes, and thus avoided any possible cause of sulks or tantrums.*

LEFT: *Illustration from the Christmas Number of 'The Graphic', 1895. At the end of the nineteenth century, fancy dress as a theme was used frequently in special numbers of the illustrated magazines, this one being part of a humorous strip cartoon story. The Red Indian costume, with all its splendour and finery, was by this date making more frequent appearances at fancy balls.*

LEFT: *Lily of the valley, 1906. Flowers as fancy dress have always been popular, probably because they enable a person to wear fashionable dress trimmed with the chosen flower and head-dress to match, as in this instance. Costumes were also designed to simulate flowers, sometimes described in books on fancy costume as 'animated flowers'.*

RIGHT: *Powder puff, about 1930. The swansdown powder puff became a fashionable toilet accessory in the 1920s, and probably its best known representation was on the orange, black, gold and white powder box created for Coty by the well known Art Deco artist Lalique. The bodice and skirt of this dress appear to be made from lamé, maybe gold, which suggests that it was intended to represent the Coty powder puff.*

tive virtue, and the crepe paper manufacturers, Dennisons, promoted their product in a series of booklets which offered many chic and inventive variations on the 'throwaway' costume idea.

Since the Second World War fancy dress has continued to be child-orientated. Children choose their own hero figures, either those with a timeless appeal to their imaginations, such as brides, princesses, witches or pirates; the leading characters from current television series or films; or the everyday life figures the children seek to emulate, such as nurses, policemen, soldiers or footballers. Many such outfits can be bought from toyshops and are used in everyday play, while for inventive mothers the advent of non-woven fabrics, fake fur, staples and PVA glue have meant that with the minimum of skill and time, almost any child's dream costume can be created.

FANCY DRESS TODAY

There was not much interest, understandably, in fancy dress during the Second World War. With shortages of practically everything and strict rationing, most people were obliged to use all their ingenuity, and create miracles of 'make do and mend' in order to have clothes for everyday life. Since the period of austerity continued for some years after the war, the first big occasion for which fancy dress seemed both possible and appropriate was the Coronation in 1953. Once again children's fancy dress parades were held at street parties and on village greens up and down Britain, and adults participated enthusiastically in fancy dress balls and pageants.

It was to be only a brief revival, however. The spread of television killed off the custom of family dressing up as

An original design for fancy dress by Dimitri Vetter, mid 1920s. Mainly a theatrical costume designer, Vetter also worked on fancy dress, and a series of designs for children's costumes is in the possession of Bermans and Nathans. 'Paint Box' or 'Artist' are instantly attractive because of the essential use of many colours.

part of home entertainment and, together with more general changes in social patterns, seemed to push into the background fancy dress on every level. Even the Chelsea Arts Ball, held annually since 1909, ceased after 1958 (although it was revived in 1984). Modern society seemed too inhibited, or too self-conscious, to enjoy fancy dress any more. The 1950s and early 1960s saw one or two lavish 'costume' balls given in Rome and Venice by South American millionaires and Italian film directors, but apart from glossy photographs in *Vogue* and the society press, they did not capture the public's imagination. Fancy dress was left strictly to the children, who took part in parades at church fetes and village carnivals, dressed predictably as the current 'hero' of television or the cinema, such characters as Davy Crockett, Batman and Darth Vader (stars respectively of the 1950s, 1960s and 1970s) achieving a mass popularity never before known.

Fancy dress, however, is by no means dead: on the contrary, it is enjoying a considerable revival in the 1980s. Perhaps it has something to do with more leisure, less desire to conform, and a general relaxation of the rules of what should be worn where and when. Many young people choose to adopt for their everyday lives an extremely individual style of dressing, and walk down the High Street in the robes of a Nepalese monk or with a Mohican Indian hairstyle. Others of all ages spend their leisure hours dressed as Cavaliers or Roundheads, or nineteenth-century canal boatmen, and imitate their way of life, so it is not surprising that in this general climate many of the less exhibitionist majority embrace the opportunity to 'do their own thing' at a party. Fancy dress hire shops are opening, and existing ones are expanding their businesses in all the major towns as proof of this trend. There must be a basic human need for such an outlet as fancy dress, and its appeal is timeless, for alongside the Spaceman, Wonderwoman and Wombles costumes hang those of Harlequin, a Chinaman, a bishop and the Devil, as popular today as they were two hundred years ago.

30

ABOVE: *Coronation Day, 2nd June 1953. As in villages throughout Britain, the inhabitants of Woolverton, Someset, joined together for a grand celebration of Coronation Day, which included a children's fancy dress parade. As well as the predictable cowboy, Indian, pirate, nurse and gypsy, the line-up also shows some topical 'Coronation' costumes: a very professional-looking guardsman, front left, a lifeguard in a delightfully home-made helmet and breastplate next to him, and, behind, a Coronation peeress, who won first prize.*

BELOW: *Hull Rugby League Football Club supporters seeing their team off to the Rugby League Cup Final at Wembley, May 1983. These lively examples of spontaneity in fancy dress are carried out in the club colours of black and white. These have been used to good effect for the whole outfit, but the hats in particular have an exuberance and inventiveness generated by the enthusiasm for the sport of Rugby League in this northern city.*

FURTHER READING

The history of fancy dress
De Marly, Diana. *Worth, Father of Haute Couture.* Elm Tree Books. 1980.
Fox, Celina, and Ribeiro, Aileen. *Masquerade.* Museum of London. 1983.
Stevenson, Sara, and Bennett, Helen. *Van Dyck in Check Trousers.* Scottish National Portrait Gallery. 1978.

The design and making of fancy dress
Aria, Mrs. *Costume: Fanciful, Historical and Theatrical.* Macmillan. 1906.
Asher, Jane. *Fancy Dress.* Pelham. 1983.
Fancy Dress. Liberty. 1890s.
Fancy Dress for Children. Liberty. 1899.
Greenhowe, Jean. *Fancy Dress for Girls.* Batsford. 1976.
Holt, Ardern. *Fancy Dresses Described.* The Queen, 1879. Debenham and Freebody, 1880.
Holt, Ardern. *Gentlemen's Fancy Dress.* Wyman, 1880. Arnold, 1898.
How to Make Crepe Paper Costumes. Dennison Manufacturing Co Ltd. 1927.
Schild, Marie. *Children's Fancy Costumes.* Miller. 1886.
Schild, Marie. *Schild's Fancy Costumes.* Miller. 1899.
Schild, Marie (editor). *Album of Fancy Costume.* Miller. 1890s.

Theatrical costumiers published their own booklets listing characters and styles of costume. The most famous of these were Burnet's, Nathan's and Simmons's. The publishers of paper patterns, in particular Butterick and Weldon, also produced catalogues of fancy dress designs. Many magazines throughout the nineteenth and twentieth centuries published articles on and illustrations of fancy dress and notable fancy dress balls. The following gave the most detailed advice and descriptions: *The Illustrated London News* (1842-); *The Queen* (1861-1970); *The Graphic* (1869-1932).

PLACES TO VISIT

The following museums have the main collections of fancy dress. The costumes will probably not be on display, therefore it is advisable to make an appointment before a visit.

Bethnal Green Museum of Childhood, Cambridge Heath Road, London E2 9PA. Telephone: 01-980 2415.
Castle Howard Costume Galleries, Castle Howard, York YO6 7DA. Telephone: Coneysthorpe (065 384) 333.
The Castle Museum, Tower Street, York YO1 1RY. Telephone: York (0904) 53611.
Costume and Fashion Research Centre, 4 Circus, Bath, Avon BA1 2EW. Telephone: Bath (0225) 61111
Merseyside County Museums, William Brown Street, Liverpool L3 8EN. Telephone: 051-207 0001 or 5451.
Museum of Costume and Textiles, 51 Castle Gate, Nottingham NG1 6AF. Telephone: Nottingham (0602) 411881.
The Museum of London, London Wall, London EC2Y 5HN. Telephone: 01-600 3699.
Shambellie House Museum of Costume, New Abbey, Dumfries. Telephone: New Abbey (038 785) 375. (Administered by the Royal Scottish Museum, Edinburgh EH1 1JF. Telephone: 031-225 7534).